# Meditation Master Rudi

# Why the Religions have Failed and not God ?

# Why don't exist Hell, Paradise, Moksha,

# Nirvana and Enlightenment ?

# Meditation Master
# Rudi Zimmerer

## Why the Religions have
## failed and not God?

### Why don't exist Hell, Paradise, Moksha, Nirvana and Enlightenment?

Author: Rudi Zimmerer
Title: Why the Religions have failed and not God?
Sub: Why don't exist Hell, Paradise, Moksha, Nirvana and Enlightenment?


ISBN-13: 9798541391596
Category: Religion & Spirit

Publisher:
Divine Success S. A.
-------------------------------------------------------------------------------------------------------

# The Intention of this book

My Intention is to help you to separate the good and useful content from the bad content of your Religion. So that it is easier to connect with God to enjoy your religious and worldly life.

Gandhi said: Religion is man-made. Gandhi had studied and analyzed all Religion and came to similar results like me.

In all religious scriptures are mistakes and many mistakes are done intentionally to exploit the people! We don't need that! For instance, slavery is allowed in the Islam, Christian and Jewish Religion!

Gandhi said: God doesn't need Religion!
This means we can even create our own Religion for ourselves and surrender to God. Or we skip the bad stuff of our chosen Religion and enjoy our life. And that no Religion wants because they lose their customers and can't suck them out anymore!

My real intention is to increase your faith in God and then your life will be much better. Read Chapter: "True Religion" /"How to develop a Love Relationship with God?"

God could not prevent the organized Religions from their:

1. Greed,

2. Power-trips,

3. Torture,

4. Killing,

5. Cheating,

6. Suppressing the people with a bad consciousness.

About me:
I never got baptized into any Religion. Still, I was a disciple of
different spiritual Masters from different Religions. I have practiced
all main Religions and know them quite well. I got adored by the
President of the Hindus for my Meditation and surrender…

Because I know all main Religion (Hindu, Taoism, Zen-Buddhism,
Osho, and Christian) I chose what I like.

I didn't find any mistakes in the I-Ging and Tao De King, only the
personal God relationship is missing. And God should be in our focus.

I love the Srimad Bhagavatam and the Gita, even they are not
flawless. For instance, everything is Destiny or Karma and we can't
change our lives. The Srimad Bhagavatam is against enjoying worldly
pleasure.

I have heard and even I agree that the Bible is one of the most negative books in the world. It describes rather more how bad people are instead to motivate us to be good! The Bible gives us a bad conscious for enjoying sex. I don't need that!

Never the less, I have never seen the greater worship of God than from the negroid African Christians. Miracles happened quite frequently when an African Healer was conducting the worship!

The Quran is and was a tool to conquer different countries. The Quran encourages to kill, torture, enslave and rape the nonbeliever of the Islam. And the Quran motivate to suppress the women. It supports and encourages the Muslim terrorists. I will describe that in my Chapter of the Islam.

The Sufism had been older than every Religion. The Sufis are going the Path of Love. Their Focus is to love God. There exist Hindu, Christian and Muslim Sufis.
In the 10th to 12th century, the Islam Sufism were blooming and developed one of the most effective spiritual paths to experience God.

Both examples of the negroid African Christian and the Sufis show us that we can develop great faith in every Religion.

Why should we not do the same?

# Contents

# How the Religions exploit the people?

All Religions who like to exploit the people teach the Hell and
Paradise. For our sins, we have to go to the Hell and for our good
deeds, we go to the Paradise. The Religions teaches what is good or
bad. After we pass by, God/Allah/Yama judging our lives and decide
how many days we go to the hell or to the paradise.
Sorry, I don't believe that there is somebody who can judge over an
entire life.
For instance, for the Hindu is a sin to kill an insect. How many sins
you have done, when killing an insect is a sin? Without killing the
insects we can't feed the world!

I wonder why slavery is allowed for the Islam and Christian Religion
(Read chapter "The Islam" and "The worst verses in the Bible").

Why is sex bad for the Christian, Hinduism, and Buddhism? (Read
chapter: "What is bad about Sex?")

Why is sex with slaves okay, even you are married and have sex with a
married slave? (Bible, Quran)

Why is it okay to sell your daughter as a sex slave? (Bible)

The Hindu and Buddhism have also the Hell and Paradise as described
before. In addition, they have a reincarnation. After visiting the Hell or
Paradise the people reincarnate in a body of an animal or human being.
Then again the people have to suffer in the world. Because life is

suffering. For the Hindu and the Buddhism is the goal never get born again. When we have done everything right in their scriptures we don't have to reincarnate. And we will end in Moksha, Mukti, or Nirvana.

How would it be to enjoy our life, then we don't be afraid of getting reborn?

After all religious scriptures besides the Taoism, we go to hell when we are not baptized in that Religion! For the Bible and Quran are all the other Religions wrong? For instance, if you are not a Muslim you are a nonbeliever and go into the hell. Or if you are not a baptized Christian you go also to Hell… Read my chapter Islam and Read: (https://en.wikipedia.org/wiki/Fate_of_the_unlearned ). What to do?

## In the wisdom of the Lao Tzu-Taoism:

Doesn't exist Paradise, Hell, Nirvana, Moksha, Mukti, Enlightenment or Reincarnation.
The death is not the end. Our souls create new souls or combine souls create a new soul.
Everywhere are living the Spirits originated from the dead.

Science proved that we can spiritual contact the dead.
How could we contact the deceased when there would be Hell and Paradise? That would be impossible!

The goals of the Taoism are a moral life with a good heart, health, and longevity. And that makes sense! See my books: "The Magic of

11

Qigong." ; "Heal yourself and stay healthy!" ; "Enjoy your life now!".

I will prove later that the Taoism is right that there exists no paradise or hell or death. Science proved through 20 minutes of the clinical death, that there is no death, paradise or hell. See Chapter: It doesn't exist the death.

For the Hindu, Christian, Buddhism is sex a sin, when we enjoy our sex and don't procreate. We are sinful if we make out of fun sex. We should even have a bad consciousness when we are enjoying sex. These Religions have a double standard because their leaders enjoy secretly sex.

What has sex to do with God? Why has God given us lust and the enjoyment of sex, when sex is bad? See my answers in the chapter, "What is bad about Sex?" Sex is good for the Taoism and Islam.

The Religions give us rules, moralities that nobody can keep and blackmail us with a bad consciousness when we can't adopt their moralities. Because the Religions wants Wealth and Power. The Religions support the establishment. And so they force us to follow the establishment and to get the money of the wealthy.

What have these corrupt Religions to do with God? They are a mafia and use even mafia methods. I will prove that.

I describe the concepts of the Religions to exploit and suppress the people!

# We start with the Christian...

The Christians exploit the people with the Hell. If you badly sin you should counteract and donate money to the church. For Instance, the Mafia donate money for their sins. And then the Mafia continue to kill. The Churches earn money from sins. So, l more sins so more money. Great business idea.

The Christian church overpowered the governments and ruled the countries. Greece was the last Country, beside the Vatican ruled from the Church.
For instance, the Philippines, the Catholic Church is making politics during the worship of God.
The Christian pressed the African slaves and the Indian to get baptized. The Indians were blackmailed with food or health care to get baptized.

On the deathbed comes the hour of trueness. The priest enters the last oiling when the patient has confessed his sins. Because of his sins, the priest demands the heritage of that dying person. Otherwise, this poor soul goes to hell. The priest exploits the dying person.
And that happened again and again in Germany until the Government partial stopped that and set up a limit of the heritage for the priest.

# The Islam

How does the Islam exploit and suppress the people?

For instance, Malaysia is a relative free Muslim Country. In Malaysia, 60% of the population are Muslims. The politicians must be Muslims. In every Id-card is written what is the Religion of that person. The Religion police of Malaysia checks the people if they taking drugs, having sex with an unmarried partner or keeping the rules of the Islam. Who breaks the religious laws get severe punishment.

In South Arabia, the Islam is much stricter and the punishment is beating, stoning, torture and cutting the neck. You can't change your Religion when you are a Muslim.
The nonbeliever of the Islam in a Muslim country has more freedom. They can drink liqueur, can stay together unmarried, or can sell beer.

With these religious rules (Sharia) the people get suppressed and threaten. The Sharia for women means a total submission. Read my Chapter: The Islam.

# The Hindu Religion

The Hindu Religion doesn't care so much about their people. Most of the Hindus have no glue of their own religious scriptures. The Hindu scripture is easy to understand and answer all kind of religious question. Read the Srimad Bhagavatam or Gita.
The Hindu system has 4 casts:
Brahmins (priestly people),
the Kshatriyas (also called Rajanyas, who were rulers, administrators,

14

and warriors),
the Vaishyas (artisans, merchants, tradesmen, and farmers),
and Shudras (laboring classes).


During our lifetime we can't change our cast nor to marry in a
different cast.
The Brahmins don't teach the other casts Religion. The Brahmins earn
their money by making worships or sacrifice for the Lord or
conducting marriage and the death. For the Brahmins is not allowed to
work. Many Brahmins live from begging.


The Hindu Religion blackmails the people with the hell and with
reincarnation.
In the Hindu religion exist so many different and complicated rules
that nobody can adapt to all rules. So everybody is sinful. And
everybody needs to go to a Brahmin to make a paid puja (worship of
God). This is good business in the famous Hindu temples.

For instance, sinful is:

1. To kill an insect or animal.

2. To jump or step over a body or musical instrument.

3. To hear or make the Ragas at the wrong time.

4. To pie in the wrong direction.

5. To have oral sex.

6. To dry cloth in the night when the cloth hangs outside.

7. To work instead to worship at certain times.

8. To take drugs, regardless which drug. Why take the Shiva devotees

hashish?

9. To marry a non-Aryan or non-Hindu or from a different cast. In Nepal are many Aryan married to Tibetan and Chinese?

10.    For the Hindus is killing a cow, one of the worst sins. Because a cow is holy. Why starving these holy cows? In Nepal the Hindus slaughter Buffaloes. Are Buffaloes are not cows? Today India is the biggest export country for beef.

# The Buddhism

The Buddhism is similar in the technique to exploit the people like the Hindus. If you go to a temple, you pay for the religious ceremonies, and when monks pray for you.
The Tibetan Buddhism is the worst exploiter of their people. I have seen that even the poorest Tibetan were sacrificing their money to the Tibetan Monks. And for these poor people was it not allowed to enter the temple, even they had built or repaired the temple. I saw the fat Tibetan monks collecting money in Sacks from the poor people in Lhasa/Tibet.

The Tibetan Monks let the poor people pay for their health treatment or praying.

The Zen Monks were selling Enlightenment certificates to their people. Even it never existed Enlightenment, see my Chapter: There exists no Enlightenment.

# The Crime of the Religions

The world would have done it better without these organized Religions.

The Organized Religions have done one war after the next. Even, the Religions made wars against different sects of their own Religion. And that is true for every Religion.

# Which is the worst Religion?

If we would compare all the abusing, cheating, lying, torture and killing of people that these organized Religions have done, it would be hard to decide whether the Christian or the Islam is the worst Religion.

The difference between the Christian Religion and the Islam are:

The Islam encourages:

1. slavery,

2. torture,

3. suppressing

4. and killing of nonbelievers.

5. The terrorists have the legitimation from Quran to kill, rape and torture. See my Chapter, "The Islam".

17

The Christians don't need the encouragement from their Bible to kill, torture or cheat in the name of God!

Never the less, we will find in every Religion religious people. So to abuse, neglect or discriminate the follower of a Religion makes no sense!

In the Buddhist Religion, Jainism, Taoism, and Jnani Yoga don't exist a personal God relationship and that is bad.

I think a personal God Relationship and the Kundalini are the best what the Religions have brought to us. Without them, a Religion would not make sense for me!

# Corruption:

## We start with the Buddhism.

The Thai Military Government is checking every Temple for corruption. Every Temple should pay Tax. Why?

For instance, one Abbot traded with skins and seldom animals under conservations.

The police tried everything to catch that wicked Abbot. The Buddhists protected him through huge demonstrations. Even famous Buddhists protect a criminal.

The donations for prestige objects or for the poor monks get in the pocket of the Abbot. I have seen that.

The Tibetan Religious people, like Rinpoches, do corruption in Nepal. A Rinpoche should be a divine incarnation. The Tibetan have blind faith in Rinpoches or the Dalai Lama. And this blind faith in the Rinpoches is misused from the Rinpoches. The Rinpoches collect money for their temples and nobody checks were the money is going. Secretly, the Rinpoches procreate kids who become the next Rinpoche. For some Rinpoches (who are in the Tantra teaching) are allowed to marry and have kids and this is not allowed for most Rinpoche.

# The Hinduism

The Hindu Gurus have been the best cheaters in the world. For instance read the book: "Holy Hell: A Memoir of Faith, Devotion, and Pure Madness".

Read my Chapter: "There exists no Enlightenment".

Osho had over 100 Rolls Royces. He was sucking out his devotees for his Rolls Royces.

Sai Baba had done his fake miracles and collected money like crazy.

Why is this possible? The "Srimad Bhagavatam" demands: It is not allowed to criticize a Guru. When the devotes of a Guru have witnessed Abusing or even small critique, they have the right to punish and even to kill that person.

# The Christian

I give here some examples, but these examples are the tip of the ice mountain.

The famous Mother Theresa got huge donations for her Calcutta project to help the needy. And most of the donations got the Catholic Church.

The Red Cross (owner Catholic Church) got over 500Million for a donation of the Tahiti earthquake. The Red Cross described in nice brochures what they have done with the money. The trueness is the Red Cross has done nearly nothing for Tahiti. Read https://www.npr.org/2015/06/03/411524156/in-search-of-the-red-cross-500-million-in-haiti-relief.

There exist different statistics about how much money of the donations are spent for that charity project. We should calculate between 1% and 5% the rest gets the Catholic Church. The official number is 92% of the donations are going to charity and that the Red Cross has never proved that. This means corruption! The same is true for the Missio Charity (owned Catholic Church).

When the pope is going to the poorest countries, he is coming back with a sack of money. Tax-free. What is the difference between a Mafia boss and the Pope? The Mafia Boss is only a small fish!

These strategies have made the Catholic Church to the biggest Real Estate owner of the world.

Even the Bible is telling us that: Money is evil. Money corrupts the people.

No one can serve two masters. Either you will hate the one and love the other, or you will be devoted to the one and despise the other. You cannot serve both God and money. Matthew 6:24

The Churches have chosen the money over God. Most of the Christians left the Churches because of their double standard!!!


# The Islam

Which are the most corrupt countries in the world? The Muslim countries, like Indonesia, Algeria, Morocco…. Because the leaders of the Muslim countries have so much power that nobody in the country can threaten them.

For instance, the Malaysia Prime Minister Najib Razak has corrupt $3

Bill. When the Parliament and the King demand that the President should resign. The Prime Minister said Allah doesn't want that. Even worse it is in South Arabia. Now King Salman found out that several $100Bill is lost through corruption. He arrested already some Billionaire.

The Islam has his own Religion Police that is checking and threaten the citizen of a Muslim Country. If the people can't keep the religious rules, the Police gets money.

For instance: A friend of mine and his friends stayed in a hotel in Malaysia. The Religion Police were checking them at 2 Am in the morning. His friends are an unmarried couple and got arrested. Because they had been unmarried and could not prove that they are Christians!!! Sure, the police wanted money!

# Sexual Abuse

The sexual abuse of kids and women in the Catholic Churches
through priests is well known. In the USA left 25% of the
Catholics the Catholic church because of the sexual abuse of
Kids and women through the Catholic priests. Even sex is not
allowed for the priests. For the Christian, sex is only allowed for
creating children, otherwise, sex is sinful.
The previous Pope Benedict XVI had to resign because he kept
all the sexual abuse of his priests, bishops, cardinals, and monks
in secret. The Pope had not opened the sexual abuse files to the
police and that is not allowed – this is a crime!


In the Islam is suppressing of his wife and raping of his own wife
allowed. Even more, it is allowed to enslave and capture women
and to rape them. See my Chapter, Islam. The Quran is
supporting sexual abuse, even for children. And that are doing
the terrorists.


For most of all Hindu sects are Sex bad. Never the less we can
read about the sexual abuse of Gurus, priests, and monks.


For the Buddhists monks is forbidden sex. For Instance, in
Thailand happen many sex scandals done by Buddhist monks,
every month.


This means celibacy has never worked for any Religion. Martin
Luther gave the priests the right to marry and have children. And
the problem with sexual abuse by the priests was over.

# Killing and Torture

# The Christian

The Christian Churches are famous for their torture and killing. For instance: Burning of witches. Millions of Innocent women got burned on the stakes of the churches.

The Churches demonized and abused the people afterward they killed them as the devil. Can you show me what torture the Christian Church didn't have made? And all in the name of God.

The Christians Religions wars are legendary. In the 30-years war in Germany (between Protestants and Catholics) were killed 25% of the population. The Crusade against the Muslim. During the WWI and WWII, the priests proved that the enemies are evil and good to kill. The command: you should not kill was transformed killing and torture is right!!

# The Islam

The Quran encourages torture, kill, enslave and rape Nonbelievers of the Islam. And so the Islam supports the terrorists. I prove that in my Chapter: "The Islam". The Islam is famous for their cruel wars, torture, and terrorists. After the Quran, it is forbidden to make wars against Muslims. Remember the wars between the Sunni Muslim and the Shiites Muslim (Iraq against Iran). Today, South Arabia makes wars together with Israel against other Muslim Countries. How can that be? The Muslims are not better than the Christians!

# The Buddhism

The Tibetan Buddhists have made many wars between the different Tibetan Buddhists sects. The Monasteries had even their own monk soldiers. Remember, the wars between the Pancha Lama and the Dalai Lama.

The Tibetan Oracle fore-casted the war in the 20th century. Then the Tibetan Church sent 48000 monks and nuns in the desert to meditate and pray until they died. That was the hugest sacrifice of human lives. The Tibetan Church used their money for buying 4000 Golden Buddhas. Instead to buy weapons. That was one of the most stupid decision ever have made.

# The Hinduism

In the Hindu Religion has been always wars against different Sects and different Religions. The religious fanatics are everywhere the same, they kill for nothing. And that is also true for the Hindu

Religion. The Indian government has done their best to pacify the different Religions in India. And today happen fewer wars and clashes.

# How authentic are the religious scriptures?

## Hindu, Buddhism, and Tao scripture:

Vyasadeva has composed a major part of The Hindu Scripture. The Brahman cast has learned them and passed orally the scriptures. There doesn't exist a proof that the Hindu scriptures are authentic because Vyasadeva didn't write them down. The same is true for the Buddhists Scriptures (Sutras), Tao Te King, I-Ging … They were not written down.

## The Bible:

The Bible got many times changed and has different versions for different sects. The Bible can't proclaim authenticity.

## The Quran should be authentic but is not authentic!

Muhammad revelations were torn in pieces and put together in the Quran without the consents of Muhammad.

The Quran was compiled in the years and decades following
Muhammad's death:
from snatches of writings on papyrus leaves,
writings on wood carvings and animal bones,
and, the memory of his companions.

There exist different versions of the Quran. The older versions of the
Quran had been destroyed or are not publicly viewable. Muhammad
spoke in an Arabic dialect and so difficult to write down in pure
Arabic.

# How can we believe in the Religious Scriptures?

How can we believe in these Religious Scriptures, when the organized
Religions had the chance to change in their favor the scripture to gain
power and money?

I will proof the organized Religions have changed in their favor the
religious scriptures!

# Why has Martin Luther translated the Bible into German?

Because the population could not properly understand the Latin of the
Bible. And the priests were teaching their likes to gain money and
power!

After Martin Luther translated the Bible, wars began between the Protestant Church and the Catholic Church.

# The Hindu scripture

In the Hindu Religion, exists different sects who proclaim that they are right and the other sects are wrong. Because every sect thinks only their deity is the almighty God and the other deities like Krishna, Kali, Shiva are worthless and sinful.

For instance, the Hari Krishna Sect defamed all other Hindu Sects who don't adore Krishna.
The Hindu Priests changes the Hindu scripture in their favor because the common man has no knowledge of the Hindu scripture.

# The Quran:

In the Islam are two different sects the Sunni Muslims and the Shiites Muslims. The Shiites Muslim proclaim that only Ali was the real Caliph (president of the Islam) and the 2 previous Caliphs had been dishonest and corrupt. The first Caliph was responsible for the Quran. The Quran got like all the other religious scriptures changed in favor of Power and Money for the Caliph.

# The Tao I-Ging and Tao de King:

The Taoism is not an organized Religion like the other Religions. The Tao scripture, I Ging and Tao de King is not in favor of money and power for the Tao priests.

# The Islam

## The Islam scriptures

As reference, I use the Noble Quran

7. The Quran is a collection of words that Muhammad attributed to Allah.

8. The Hadith is a collection of narrations of the life and deeds of Muhammad.

9. The Sira is his recorded biography.

10.    The Sunnah is Muhammad's way of life, on which Islamic law (Sharia) is based.

The Quran (Koran) is the Holy Book of Islam and the religion's most sacred text. The word itself means "recitation." It is a series of "revelations" that Muhammad claimed to have received from Allah.

The Quran has 114 Suras (chapters) that contain the ayat (verses). The Suras are not in chronological or thematic sequence or logical continuity. The Suras sorted out by general size. The larger Suras appearing first.

The Suras of the Quran are mainly from his Mecca time and Medina time.

In his Mecca time, Muhammad could not force the Islam with violence on others, so he was interpreting the stories of the Bible and Torah.

In Muhammad's Medina time, the Suras became fanatic, intolerant and commanding for war against other Religions. So stronger military Muhammad got so more violent he became. The bloody 9ht Sura (the verse of the sword) proofs that.

The biggest part of the Quran discriminates between Believer in the Islam and Nonbeliever. To abandon the Islam is the worst or to criticize the Quran. The punishment for that is death.

# Muslim Marriage:

The husband is responsible for his wives (4 women are possible) and has to give the supply to her. The wife can only have one husband. The females are forbidden in the Mosque, and they must be veiled in public.
The divorce is possible for both.
After the divorce, the kids are going to the husband.
When the husband or wife have made adultery (Zina), both can forgive each other or can divorce.

# How to prove a liaison in the Muslim marriage?

The wife/husband needs 4 male witnesses who have seen the penetration to prove the sexual affair. Or the person confess 4 times the sexual penetration with another partner!

Is it possible to have an affair without 4 male witnesses have seen the penetration or to confess?

After Maliki legal school: the single woman pregnancy is proof of adultery. This can mean, if an unmarried woman got raped and can't prove that she got raped, then she has done adultery!

# Possible punishment for adultery (Zina) is stoning.

After the Hadith for Zina:
The proof for this is that the Prophet did not seek out the married
woman whom Mâ`iz committed fornication with. He did not inquire
after her husband and command him to divorce her. All he said was:
"O Unays, go to that man's wife, and if she confesses, then have her
stoned." [Sahîh al-Bukhârî (6633) and Sahîh Muslim (1698)]

Adultery has nothing to do with the country laws. Adultery is an
offense of the Islam and will be punished through the Islam. When
there was an evidence of the affair, the Prophet said: "The child
belongs to the (marriage) bed, and the adulterer is stoned." [Sahîh al-
Bukhârî (2053) and Sahîh Muslim (1457)]

What is about prostitution? The husband marries the prostitute,
penetrates her and afterward divorces her. This is the standard practice
in Saudi Arabia. The Quran allows it to get married 3 times with the
same spouse.

# Beat your wife until she obey!

Quran (4:34) - "Men are the maintainers of women because Allah has
made some of them excel others and because they spend out of their
property; the good women are therefore obedient, guarding the unseen
as Allah has guarded; and (as to) those on whose part you fear
desertion, admonish them, and leave them alone in the sleeping-places
and beat them; then if they obey you, do not seek a way against them;
surely Allah is High, Great." Contemporary translations sometimes
water down the word 'beat', but it is the same one used in verse 8:12
and clearly means 'to strike'.

Quran (2:228) - "and the men are a degree above them"

Quran (38:44) - "And take in your hand a green branch and beat her with it, and do not break your oath..." Allah telling Job to beat his wife (Tafsir).

Quran (33:59) - "Tell thy wives and thy daughters and the women of the believers to draw their cloaks close round them..." Men determine how women dress.

Quran (33:33) - "And abide quietly in your homes..." Women are confined to their homes except when they have permission to go out.

## Your wife should do everything to fulfill your sexual desires!!

Quran (2:223) - "Your wives are as a tilth unto you; so approach your tilth when or how ye will." Wives are to be sexually available to their husbands in all ways at all times. They serve their husbands at his command. This verse is believed to refer to anal sex (see Bukhari 60:51) and was "revealed" when women complained to Muhammad about the practice. The phrase "when and how you will" means that they lost their case.

Sahih Bukhari (72:715) - A woman came to Muhammad and begged him to stop her husband from beating her. Her skin was bruised so badly that it is described as being "greener" than the green veil she was wearing. Muhammad did not admonish her husband but instead ordered her to return to him and submit to his sexual desires.

Sahih Bukhari (72:715) - "Aisha said, 'I have not seen any woman suffering as much as the believing women'" Muhammad's own wife complained Muslim women were abused worse than other women.

## This means that the Quran makes it easy to rape women...

Why women should veil their faces. Because of the lust of the men.
Why should not the men be punished for raping?
If the man is greedy for sex and rapes a woman, he should be punished.
Why should be the women punished by wearing a veil for the lust of the man?

# The Islam allows Slavery and including Sex slavery!

Muslims should live in the way of the Prophet. Muhammed was a slave owner and trader!

The Prophet captured slaves in his wars against Nonbeliever, he had sex with them. So the Quran supports Sex slaves and makes sure that every Muslim understand that in many verses. That is more mentioned than to pray 5 times!!!

Quran (33:50):

O Prophet! We have made lawful to thee thy wives to whom thou hast paid their dowers; and those (slaves) whom thy right hand possesses out of the prisoners of war whom Allah has assigned to thee.

**The Muslim and also the ISIS can have unlimited women as sex slaves, even the Muslims are married. The Sultan of Turkey had 5000 wives! A war is good for the Muslim men.**

Quran (33:50) - "O Prophet! We have made lawful to thee thy wives to whom thou hast paid their dowers; and those (slaves) whom thy right hand possesses out of the prisoners of war whom Allah has assigned to thee.

Similar is Quran (70:29-30).

Quran (4:24) - "And all married women (are forbidden unto you) save those (captives) whom your right hands possess."

# Even sex with married slaves is permissible.

Quran (8:69) - "But (now) enjoy what ye took in war, lawful and good". The Muslim slave master may enjoy his "catch" because (according to verse 71) "Allah gave you mastery over them."

Quran (24:32) - "And marry those among you who are single and those who are fit for your male slaves and your female slaves..."

# Produce slaves...

Quran (2:178) - "O ye who believe! Retaliation is prescribed for you in the matter of the murdered; the freeman for the freeman, and the slave for the slave, and the female for the female."

**Retaliation is demanded instead of compassion. And a slave is less than a Freeman...**

Quran (16:75) - "Allah sets forth the Parable (of two men: one) a slave under the dominion of another; He has no power of any sort; and (the other) a man on whom We have bestowed goodly favours from Ourselves, and he spends thereof (freely), privately and publicly: are the two equal? (By no means;) praise is to Allah.'


**That is the confirmation that a slave is not equal than a Muslim who had captured the slave.**

# Does Islam allow freedom of Religion?

# Kill, who turns away from the Islam!

Quran (4:89) - "They wish that you reject Faith, as they have rejected (Faith), and thus that you all become equal (like one another). So take not Auliya' (protectors or friends) from them, till they emigrate in the Way of Allah (to Muhammad). But if they turn back (from Islam), take (hold) of them and kill them wherever you find them, and take neither Auliya' (protectors or friends) nor helpers from them."

# Freedom is to be Muslim or to get executed.

Quran (9:11-12) - "But if they repent and establish worship and pay the poor-due, then are they your brethren in religion. We detail Our revelations for a people who have knowledge. And if they break their pledges after their treaty (hath been made with you) and assail your religion, then fight the heads of disbelief -

Even more clear makes it the Hadith:
Sahih Bukhari (52:260) - "...The Prophet said, 'If somebody (a Muslim) discards his religion, kill him.' "

If Muslims are fighting against your Religion and people, you become a Muslim or get slaughtered or enslaved...

Sahih Bukhari (83:37) - "Allah's Apostle never killed anyone except in one of the following three situations: (1) A person who killed somebody unjustly, was killed (in Qisas,) (2) a married person who committed illegal sexual intercourse and (3) a man who fought against Allah and His Apostle and deserted Islam and became an apostate."

Sahih Bukhari (84:57) - [In the words of] "Allah's Apostle, 'Whoever changed his Islamic religion, then kill him.'"

# Kill them if they believe in different versions of the Islam.

Remember the wars between the Sunni Muslims and the Shiites Muslims.

Sahih Bukhari (89:271) - A man who embraces Islam, then reverts to Judaism is to be killed according to "the verdict of Allah and his apostle."

Sahih Bukhari (84:58) - "There was a fettered man beside Abu Muisa. Mu'adh asked, 'Who is this (man)?' Abu Musa said, 'He was a Jew and became a Muslim and then reverted back to Judaism.' Then Abu Musa requested Mu'adh to sit down but Mu'adh said, 'I will not sit down till he has been killed. This is the judgment of Allah and His Apostle (for such cases) and repeated it thrice.' Then Abu Musa ordered that the man is killed, and he was killed. Abu Musa added, 'Then we discussed the night prayers'"

Sahih Bukhari (84:64-65) - "Allah's Apostle: 'During the last days there will appear some young foolish people who will say the best words but their faith will not go beyond their throats (i.e. they will have no faith) and will go out from (leave) their religion as an arrow goes out of the game. So, wherever you find them, kill them, for whoever kills them shall have reward on the Day of Resurrection.'"

# If you believe but don't put your religion into practice, the Muslims will kill you!!!

Sahih Bukhari (11:626) - "The Prophet said, 'No prayer is harder for the hypocrites than the Fajr and the 'Isha' prayers and if they knew the reward for these prayers at their respective times, they would certainly present themselves (in the mosques) even if they had to crawl.' The Prophet added, 'Certainly, I decided to order the Mu'adh-dhin (call-maker) to pronounce Iqama and order a man to lead the prayer and then take a fire flame to burn all those who had not left their houses so far for the prayer along with their houses'."

## The fanaticism of the Muslims originates from the Quran.

# Become Muslim or the Muslim will Kill You!

The Muslim Terrorists get the permission and encouragement from the Quran to kill Nonbelievers of the Islam!!

Muslims should fight unbelievers:
until they are either dead,
converted to Islam,
or in a permanent state of subjugation under Muslim domination.

## People from different Faiths are not allowed in an Islam society.

Quran (8:38-39) - "Say to those who have disbelieved, if they cease (from disbelief) their past will be forgiven... And fight them until there is no more Fitnah (disbelief and polytheism: i.e. worshipping others besides Allah) and the religion (worship) will all be for Allah Alone [in the whole of the world ]. But if they cease (worshipping others besides Allah), then certainly, Allah is All-Seer of what they do."

**The results we see in Asia. In Pakistan, Bangladesh and Afghanistan are the Terror organizations!!**

Quran (9:29) - "Fight those who believe not in Allah nor the Last Day, nor hold that forbidden which hath been forbidden by Allah and His Messenger, nor acknowledge the religion of Truth, (even if they are) of the People of the Book, until they pay the Jizya with willing submission, and feel themselves subdued." Suras 9 and 5 are the last major chapters that Muhammad narrated - hence abrogating what came before, including the oft-quoted verse 2:256 -"There is no compulsion in religion...".

Quran (9:5) "But when the forbidden months are past, then fight and slay the Pagans wherever ye find them, and seize them, beleaguer them, and lie in wait for them in every stratagem (of war); but if they repent, and establish regular prayers and practice regular charity, then open the way for them..."

Quran (2:193) - "And fight them until fitna is no more, and religion is only of Allah. But if they desist, then let there be no hostility except against wrong-doers." The key phrase here is to fight until "religion be only for Allah."

Qur'an (3:83) - "Are they seeking a religion other than Allah's, when every soul in the Paradises and the earth has submitted to Him, willingly or by compulsion?" But didn't the earlier verse (2:256) state that there is "no compulsion in religion"? This contradiction is resolved by abrogation - where the later verse supersedes the earlier one.

If this is not proof enough, The Hadith and Sira make it clear: **Kill the Non- Muslim!!!**

Sahih Muslim (1:33) The Messenger of Allah said: "I have been commanded to fight against people till they testify that there is no god but Allah, that Muhammad is the messenger of Allah, and they establish prayer and pay zakat." To be safe, people must profess faith in Allah (the shahada) and follow Islamic practices (the zakat and salat). Violence is thus sanctioned until the victims embrace Muhammad's religion and become obedient, practicing Muslims.

Sahih Muslim (19:4294) - "When you meet your enemies who are polytheists (which includes Christians), invite them to three courses of action. If they respond to any one of these, you also accept it and withhold yourself from doing them any harm. Invite them to (accept) Islam; if they respond to you, accept it from them and desist from fighting against them ... If they refuse to accept Islam, demand from them the Jizya. If they agree to pay, accept it from them and hold off your hands. If they refuse to pay the tax, seek Allah's help and fight them"

**There are only three choices in Islam:**
**Either submit, or live under the suzerainty of Islam, or die."**
**(source: The al-Qaeda)**

Sahih Bukhari (8:387) - "Allah's Apostle said, 'I have been ordered to fight the people till they say: 'None has the right to be worshipped but Allah.' And if they say so, pray like our prayers, face our Qibla and slaughter as we slaughter, then their blood and property will be sacred to us and we will not interfere with them except legally and their reckoning will be with Allah.'"

# Become Muslim or we take your property!!

Sahih Bukhari (53:392) - "While we were in the Mosque, the Prophet came out and said, "Let us go to the Jews" We went out till we reached Bait-ul-Midras. He said to them, "If you embrace Islam, you will be safe. You should know that the earth belongs to Allah and His Apostle, and I want to expel you from this land. So, if anyone amongst you owns some property, he is permitted to sell it, otherwise, you should know that the Earth belongs to Allah and His Apostle."

Sahih Bukhari (2:24) - "Allah's Apostle said: "I have been ordered (by Allah) to fight against the people until they testify that none has the right to be worshipped but Allah and that Muhammad is Allah's Apostle, and offer the prayers perfectly and give the obligatory charity, so if they perform a that, then they save their lives and property from me except for Islamic laws and then their reckoning (accounts) will be done by Allah."

# Force them to become Muslim or kill them!

Sahih Bukhari (60:80) - "The Verse:--'You (true Muslims) are the best of peoples ever raised up for mankind.' means, the best of peoples for the people, as you bring them with chains on their necks till they embrace Islam."

Sahih Bukhari (59:643) - "Testify that none has the right to be worshipped except Allah, or else I will chop off your neck!" Words of a military leader who Muhammad sent on an expedition with the mission of destroying a local religion in Yemen.

# All People should be Muslim!!!

Ibn Kathir (Commenting on Quran 2:256 in the unabridged version of his tafsir) - "Therefore all people of the world should be called to Islam. If anyone of them refuses to do so, or refuses to pay the jizya, they should be fought till they are killed."

# Islam loves torture

This chapter tells you everything how brutal and rude the Islam is!!!

Quran (5:33) - "The punishment of those who wage war against Allah and His messenger and strive to make mischief in the land is only this, that they should be murdered or crucified or their hands and their feet should be cut off on opposite sides..." Quran (8:12) - "Remember thy Lord inspired the angels (with the message): "I am with you: give firmness to the Believers: I will instill terror into the hearts of the Unbelievers: smite ye above their necks and smite all their finger-tips off them."

Quran (48:29) - "Muhammad is the messenger of Allah. And those with him are hard against the disbelievers and merciful among themselves"

Quran (24:2) - "The woman and the man guilty of adultery or fornication,- flog each of them with a hundred stripes: Let not compassion move you." Not only is physical torture prescribed as punishment for moral crime between consenting adults, but believers are told to suppress their natural urge for human compassion.

Quran (22:19-22) - "These twain (the believers and the disbelievers) are two opponents who contend concerning their Lord. But as for those who disbelieve, garments of fire will be cut out for them; boiling fluid will be poured down on their heads. Whereby that which is in their bellies, and their skins too, will be melted; And for them are hooked rods of iron. Whenever, in their anguish, they would go forth from thence they are driven back therein and (it is said unto them): Taste the doom of burning." The punishment of those who merely disbelieve in Muhammad's claims about himself is described as being horrifically brutal in many other places as well, such as Quran 4:56, which says that they will face a continuous cycle of torture in which their skin will be burned off only to be replaced by new skin.

Hadith:
Sahih Bukhari (52:261) - "[Muhammad] had their hands and feet cut off. Then he ordered for nails which were heated and passed over their eyes, and whey were left in the Harra (i.e. rocky land in Medina). They asked for water, and nobody provided them with water till they died." Muhammad had two killers put to death, not in the way of "an eye-for-an-eye," but in a more agonizing manner. (See also Sahih Bukhari 4:234) and Sahih Muslim (16:4131): "They were caught and brought to him (the Holy Prophet). He commanded them, and (thus) hands and feet were cut off and their eyes were gouged and then they were thrown in the sun until they died.")

Sahih Muslim (17:4196) - A married man confesses that he has adultery (four times, as required). Muhammad orders him planted in the ground and pelted with stones. According to the passage, the first several stones caused such pain that he tried to escape and was dragged back.

Ibn Ishaq 764 - After amassing a powerful army, Muhammad sent his forces to take the peaceful farming community of Khaybar by surprise. In the aftermath, he was dissatisfied with the amount of plunder and felt that the town's treasurer, Kinana, might be holding out on him. He had the man brought to him:

When he [Muhammad] asked him about the rest he refused to produce it, so the apostle gave orders to al-Zubayr bin al-Awwam, "Torture him until you extract what he has." So he kindled a fire with flint and steel on his chest until he was nearly dead. Then the apostle delivered him to Muhammad bin Maslama and he struck off his head."

(As a happy side note to the story – Kinana's untimely death left a beautiful young widow named Saffiya, whom Muhammad was then able to "marry").

# Don't be a friend of Jewish and Christian

Quran (5:51) - "O you who believe! do not take the Jews and the
Christians for friends; they are friends of each other, and whoever
amongst you takes them for a friend, then surely he is one of them;
surely Allah does not guide the unjust people."
Quran (5:80) - "You will see many of them befriending those who
disbelieve; certainly evil is that which their souls have sent before for
them, that Allah became displeased with them and in chastisement
shall they abide." Those Muslims who befriend unbelievers will abide
in hell.

Quran (3:28) - "Let not the believers Take for friends or helpers
Unbelievers rather than believers: if any do that, in nothing will there
be help from Allah: except by way of precaution, that ye may Guard
yourselves against them..." Renowned scholar Ibn Kathir states that
"believers are allowed to show friendship outwardly, but never
inwardly."

Quran (3:118) - "O you who believe! do not take for intimate friends
from among others than your own people, they do not fall short of
inflicting loss upon you; they love what distresses you; vehement
hatred has already appeared from out of their mouths, and what their
breasts conceal is greater still; indeed, We have made the
communications clear to you, if you will understand."

Quran (9:23) - "O ye who believe! Choose not your fathers nor your
brethren for friends if they take pleasure in disbelief rather than faith.
Whoso of you taketh them for friends, such are wrong-doers" Even
family members are not to be taken as friends if they do not accept
Islam.

Quran (53:29) - "Therefore shun those who turn away from Our
Message and desire nothing but the life of this world."

Quran (3:85) - "And whoever desires a religion other than Islam, it shall not be accepted from him, and in the hereafter, he shall be one of the losers."

# Who do not believe in Muhammad are the fuel for the hell!!

Quran (3:10) - "(As for) those who disbelieve, surely neither their wealth nor their children shall avail them in the least against Allah, and these it is who are the fuel of the fire." Those who do not believe in Muhammad are but fuel for the fire of Hell (also 66:6, 2:24. 21:98).

Quran (7:44) - "The Companions of the Garden will call out to the Companions of the Fire: "We have indeed found the promises of our Lord to us true: Have you also found Your Lord's promises true?" They shall say, "Yes"; but a crier shall proclaim between them: "The curse of Allah is on the wrong-doers" Muslims in Paradise will amuse themselves by looking down on non-Muslims in Hell and mocking them while they are being tortured (see 22:19-22).

Quran (1:5-7) - "Show us the straight path, The path of those whom Thou hast favored; Not the (path) of those who earn Thine anger nor of those who go astray" This is a prayer that Muslims are to repeat each day. "Those who earn Thine anger" refers to Jews; "those who go astray" refers to Christians (see Sahih Bukhari (12:749) and Sahih Muslim 34:6448)).

# Muhammed's Biography

"Muhammed is a narcissist, a pedophile, a mass murderer,
a terrorist, a misogynist, a lecher, a cult leader, a madman
a rapist, a torturer, an assassin and a looter."

A quote from former Muslim Ali Sina, who offered $50,000 to
anyone who could prove this wrong based on Islamic texts.

The reward has gone unclaimed.

Imagine....

A rich guy, living from trading, got some revelation of God. That
is in the spiritual scene not unusual. Mainly, Muhammed
revelations were about him.

In Tibet, the Medium trained for spiritual revelation over 20 years
in secluding. Otherwise, that Medium would not be pure enough.
Because all that we receive as a channel will our Ego distort. Or
even worse can be a devil spirit. We should check every flattering
from our ego that is coming from that channel. Because it can be
a devil spirit or our ego. We should check our channel from a
spiritual master or high spiritual being, as I have done it!!! I have
watched at least 4 people who went mad through channeling.

Imagine a rich guy is seizing property, kills people, rapes kids and
enslaves people. Do you think that these deeds are divine?

If a Religion suppresses the women, is this an act of love and compassion?

Imagine a prophet declares: it is the right of the conquerer to kill, enslave and rape nonbeliever. Do you think that these revelations are holly?
What kind of revelations that are?
The Revelations of a cruel conquerer or of a saint? See chapter Quran.

When the Quran is composed by a true saint, then the ISIS is right to kill, enslave people and rape women and kids!

For me is Religion love and compassion, instead to kill, rape, torture and enslave the people.

# Muhammed's Biography:

In 610, an Arab salesman with a charismatic personality attracted a small cult of fanatics. He claimed to be a prophet. Muhammed told revelations that even contradict itself. He manipulated his follower as we have seen in other sects, like the Moon sect, Hari Krishna sect.

Muhammed demanded:

11.   to steal,

12.   to lie for him

13.   to give their kids for sexual pleasure to him.

14.     The same we have also seen from these other sects.

Muhammed proclaims himself a prophet in the same lineage as
Abraham and Jesus. In his revelations, later published as Quran
he demands total obedience to him. We can read that at least 20
times is this in Quran.

Mecca, the birthplace of Muhammed was a religious, pilgrim city.
Mecca has a meteorite that was adored by different religious
groups.
The people of Mecca lived well from the pilgrims and accepted
all kinds of Religions.

In Mecca, Muhammed started to preach his Islam.
After some time, Muhammed abused different beliefs and got
trouble from the locals. Still, he had his uncle Abu Talib until 619
as a protector against the Meccan leadership.

Abu Sufyan went to Abu Talib and said: "Please let us find peace
between Muhammed on our Beliefs. We have our beliefs and he
should keep his beliefs".

Muhammed didn't agree and so he went to Medina to make wars
against Mecca.

570 - Born in Mecca
576 - Orphaned upon the death of the mother
595 - Marries Kadijah - older, wealthy widow
610 - Reports first revelations at age of 40

619 - Protector uncle dies
622 - Emigrates from Mecca to Medina (the Hijra)
623 - Orders raids on Meccan caravans
624 - Battle of Badr (victory)
624 - Evicts Qaynuqa Jews from Medina
624 - Orders assassination of Abu Afak
624 - Orders assassination of Asma bint Marwan
624 - Orders the assassination of Ka'b al-Ashraf
625 - Battle of Uhud (defeat)
625 - Evicts Nadir Jews
627 - Battle of the Trench (victory)
627 - Massacre of the Qurayza Jews
628 - Signing of the Treaty of Hudaibiya with Mecca
628 - Destruction and subjugation of the Khaybar Jews
629 - Orders first raid into Christian lands at Muta (defeat)
630 - Conquers Mecca by surprise (along with other tribes)
631 - Leads the second raid into Christian territory at Tabuk (no
battle)
632 - Dies

# The worst verses in the Bible

**In the Bible, we read:**

1. how bad the people are,

2. how bad is sex,

3. when to rape,

4. how to deal with slaves,

5. discrimination against women, and homosexuality,

6. and even about killing as necessary!

# Some of the worse verses:

1 Timothy 2:12:
St Paul's advice, women can't teach men in the church:
"I do not permit a woman to teach or to have authority over a
man; she must be silent."

In this verse, Samuel orders genocide against a neighboring
people:
"This is what the Lord Almighty says... 'Now go and strike
Amalek and devote to destruction all that they have. Do not
spare them, but kill both man and woman, child and infant, ox
and sheep, camel and donkey.'" (1 Samuel 15:3)

A command of Moses:
Exodus 22:18:
"Do not allow a sorceress to live."

Romans 1:27:
St Paul condemns homosexuality in the opening chapter of the
Book of Romans:
"In the same way also the men, giving up natural intercourse
with women were consumed with passion for one another. Men
committed shameless acts with men and received in their own
persons the due penalty for their error."

# Abusing sexuality

2 Corinthians 12:21:
21 I am afraid that when I come again my God will humble me
before you, and I will be grieved over many who have sinned
earlier and have not repented of the impurity, sexual sin, and
debauchery in which they have indulged.

Ephesians 5:3:
3 But among you, there must not be even a hint of sexual
immorality, or of any kind of impurity, or of greed because these
are improper for God's holy people.

Galatians 5:19
19 The acts of the flesh are obvious: sexual immorality,
impurity, and debauchery;

Hebrews 13:44
Marriage should be honored by all, and the marriage bed kept
pure, for God will judge the adulterer and all the sexually
immoral.

For sure that these verses are wrong and lead to a perverse sex.
Remember all these Sex scandals from the clerical.

# About Raping:

There are several passages in the Old Testament about Raping:
In Genesis 34, Dinah is abducted by Shechem in a passage that is
often interpreted as rape.
[6][7] In Numbers 31:15-18, Moses, after exacting revenge on
the Midianites, commands his army:
to kill all the boys and every non-virgin woman,
to "save for [themselves]" every virgin woman."
This means to rape all the virgin women.
How to find out whether a woman is a virgin or not? This means
to sleep with every woman. If she was not a virgin, kill her!!!

[4][8] Deuteronomy 21:10-14 presents laws regarding marrying
a captive woman. This means to have sex with her without
having her compliance.

[4][9] Judges 19:22-26 depicts Gibeah and the Levite
Concubine, in which a man sends out his concubine to a group of
angry men, where they gang rape her.[10]
Afterwards, the man cuts up the body of his concubine into
twelve pieces and sends them to the Twelve Tribes of
Israel.[4][11] 2
How brutal!!!


Samuel 13:1-14 involves the rape of Tamar.[12][13]


# About slavery:

# The old and new Testament allows slavery.

A Slave doesn't have any rights. Everything can do the master
with the slave. For instance, the master can
rape,
castrate (the French did so; see link www.goo.gl/WuAqe8),
and punish without to kill the slave.


Only a male Hebrew Slave should be released after 6 years.


## A slave can be traded like a livestock:


Leviticus 25:44-46 NLT
However, you may purchase male or female slaves from among
the foreigners who live among you. You may also purchase the
children of such resident foreigners, including those who have

been born in your land. You may treat them as your property, passing them on to your children as a permanent inheritance. You may treat your slaves like this, but the people of Israel, your relatives, must never be treated this way.

What about the male Hebrew Slave?

Exodus 21:2-6 NLT:
If you buy a Hebrew slave, he has to serve for only six years. Set him free in the seventh year, and he will owe you nothing for his freedom. If he was single when he became your slave and then married afterward, only he will go free in the seventh year. But if he was married before he became a slave, then his wife will be freed with him. If his master gave him a wife while he was a slave, and they had sons or daughters, then the man will be free in the seventh year, but his wife and children will still belong to his master. But the slave may plainly declare, 'I love my master, my wife, and my children. I would rather not go free.' If he does this, his master must present him before God. Then his master must take him to the door and publicly pierce his ear with an awl. After that, the slave will belong to his master forever.

How to get a male Hebrew slave to become permanent? Keep his wife and children, hostage, until he says he wants to become a permanent slave. What kind of family values are these?

## Sex slavery is allowed! Even it is

# allowed to sell your daughter as a sex slave!

Exodus 21:7-11 NLT:
When a man sells his daughter as a slave, she will not be freed at
the end of six years as the men are. If she does not please the
man who bought her, he may allow her to be bought back again.
But he is not allowed to sell her to foreigners, since he is the one
who broke the contract with her. And if the slave girl's owner
arranges for her to marry his son, he may no longer treat her as a
slave girl, but he must treat her as his daughter. If he himself
marries her and then takes another wife, he may not reduce her
food or clothing or fail to sleep with her as his wife. If he fails in
any of these three ways, she may leave as a free woman without
making any payment.

A man can buy as many sex slaves as he wants as long as he
feeds them, clothes them, and has sex with them!

# What does the Bible say about beating slaves?

Exodus 21:20-21 NAB:
When a man strikes his male or female slave with a rod so hard
that the slave dies under his hand, he shall be punished. If,
however, the slave survives for a day or two, he is not to be
punished, since the slave is his own property.

# Did Jesus had a different view of slavery?

No, slavery is approved in the New Testament.
The slavery of the African people in America was allowed after the New and Old Testament.


Ephesians 6:5 NLT
Slaves, obey your earthly masters with deep respect and fear. Serve them sincerely as you would serve Christ.


1 Timothy 6:1-2 NLT
Christians who are slaves should give their masters full respect so that the name of God and his teaching will not be shamed. If your master is a Christian, that is no excuse for being disrespectful. You should work all the harder because you are helping another believer by your efforts. Teach these truths, Timothy, and encourage everyone to obey them. (1 Timothy 6:1-2 NLT)


## Jesus approved of the beating of slaves, even if they didn't know they were doing anything wrong.


Luke 12:47-48 NLT:

The servant will be severely punished, for though he knew his duty, he refused to do it. "But people who are not aware that they are doing wrong will be punished only lightly. Much is required from those to whom much is given, and much more is required from those to whom much more is given."

# There are no Death, Paradise or Hell

## There is no Death

I can't die, I am Energy…

the last words of A. Einstein.

That is recently proved by the University of Berlin. Later comes the proof.

Inside of our body is the life force or life energy when we alive. When we pass by, what happens with this energy? We can't destroy energy. We (our energy) leave our body, as soul/mind. This means we get rid of this false identification with our body and become the spirit again.

And this is also my experience. I was three times clinical dead. When I passed by, I remembered the Golden Moments in my life in very intensive pictures. I saw my body from the perspective of a bird, nothing to bother about. I could even enjoy it, and last time I didn't want to come back. Because I felt so free and no worries.

## For what we have a fear of death?

The Germans scientists had simulated the death of many people with drugs.

# The science Proof:

Berlin | A team of psychologists and medical doctors associated with the Technische Universität of Berlin, have announced this morning that they had proven by clinical experimentation, the existence of some form of life after death.

This surprising announcement is based on the conclusions of a study using a new type of medically supervised near-death experiences, that allow patients to be clinically dead for almost 20 minutes before being brought back to life.

This controversial process that was repeated on 944 volunteers over that last four years necessitates a complex mixture of drugs, destined to allow the body to survive the state of clinical death and the reanimation process without damage. The body of the subject was then put into a temporary comatic state.

Most common memories include a feeling of detachment from the body, feelings of levitation, total serenity, security, warmth, the experience of absolute dissolution, and the presence of an overwhelming light.

The scientists say that they are well aware the many of their conclusions could shock a lot of people, like the fact that the religious beliefs of the various subjects seem to have held no incidence at all, on the sensations and experiences that they described at the end of the experiment. Indeed, the volunteers counted in their ranks some members are a variety of Christian churches, Muslims, Jews, Hindus, and atheists.

"I know our results could disturb the beliefs of many people", says Mr. Ackermann. "But in a way, we have just answered one of the greatest questions in the history of mankind, so I hope these people will be able to forgive us. Yes, there is life after death, and it looks like this applies to everyone."

# There are no Paradise or Hell

After the Buddhism, Christian, and Islam when somebody passed by then he goes within a short time to Hell or Paradise.

The University of Berlin put around 1000 people for 20 minutes in a clinical death.

After the research of the University, exist no Death, no Hell, and no Paradise. And there were no different results for the different Religions after the death!

The same is saying the Lao Tzu Taoism, that there is no Death, no Hell, and no Paradise. (Read Chapter: "How the Religions exploit the people.").

Why have the Religions created Paradise and Hell?

1. The Religions like to give the people a bad conscience when they make something sinful. What is sinful that decide the Religion!
2. The Religions, like Christian, Jewish, and Hindu preached that sex is sinful and perverted so the people.
3. The Religions like to blackmail the people with their bad consciousness and so to exploit them!
4. The Religions are preaching morality that they never lived by themselves. And this double standard had not improved the people.

5. The Religion want to reward people who surrender to their
   Religion.

# How would it be if we enjoy our life here on this planet?

After the Buddhism, Christian, and Islam when somebody passed by then he goes within a short time to Hell or Paradise.
The University of Berlin put nearly 1000 people for 20 minutes in a clinical death.
After the research of the University, exist no Death, no Hell, and no Paradise. And there were no different results for the different Religions after the death!
The same is saying the Lao Tzu Taoism, that there are no Death, no Hell, and no Paradise. (See Chapter 2).

Why have the Religions created Paradise and Hell?

1. The Religions like to give the people a bad conscience when they
   make something sinful. What is sinful that decide the
   Religion!
2. The Religions, like Christian, Jewish, and Hindu  preached that sex
   is sinful and perverted so the people
3. The Religions like to blackmail the people with their bad
   consciousness and so to exploit them!
4. The Religions are preaching morality that they never lived by
   themselves. And this double standard had not improved the
   people.
5. The Religion want to reward people who surrender to their
   Religion.

# How would it be if we enjoy our life here on this planet?

# There are no Enlightenment, Nirvana, or Moksha

## Is Enlightenment just another scam?

You wake up in the morning and find yourself in a different world that you cannot comprehend. Everything that you believed for many years seems wrong. The famous masters and saints: a scam? You shake your head and think "my ego is tricking me..."

After some days, your doubts come back, and you remember all the bizarre things you experienced in holy places with supposedly holy people... You feel that despite your alleged enlightenment at their hands, you are still possessed by a dark negative power, and you think, "I am getting mad..."

Then you see a video from Jimmy Rogers, the legendary fund manager. He tells you to question everything... and after 10 years, you realize most of the things you believed are wrong, and you began with false assumptions.

Now your soul is on fire... and you get all the books, all the information about the famous gurus... (See them at the end). And you praise Jimmy Rogers!

This has happened to me; I'm a guy who has spent over 10 years in Meditation retreats, have been blessed by the President of the Hindus during his meditation and his surrender. It is so heartbreaking to remember that I was the disciple of so many famous gurus in India...

# What is enlightenment?

When someone receives enlightenment, his ego will be destroyed, and it will be transformed into the divine. Afterward, his whole life emerges as the divine, and he acts in complete selflessness because he has no Ego anymore! His sex is transformed, and he is one with God, or he is God by himself.

Bhagwan, or Osho, was the Indian spiritual Master who brought the idea of enlightenment to the Western world. He described enlightenment as the greatest thing a human being could achieve in his lifetime. Bhagwan himself had already transcended beyond it...

In the last months of his life, Osho (Bhagwan) finally admitted that the Ego could not be destroyed, only "observed." This meant there really never existed any enlightenment.

Krishnamurthy, who was internationally praised as an enlightenment master, also said that there is no enlightenment.

The famous Sri Aurobindo said that so long as we have a body, we have an Ego.

The Srimad Bhagavatam said, "There exists nobody on this planet who doesn't have all three Gunas." All three Gunas are together with our ego. We can only improve our ego.

And there is nothing further mentioned about enlightenment in the Srimad Bhagavatam, nor in other religious books, like the Bible, Tao De King, I-Qing, the Quran, or the famous Sufi book: The Conference of the Birds.

Ramakrishna said we can't kill this rascal of our Ego. Instead, we use our Ego to serve God. Ramakrishna remained humble his whole life, and he served his devotees well.

# Why can't we destroy our Ego or a part of our Ego?

Our ego is hard-wired into our brain and our whole body. Regardless of what we are doing, our Ego is involved. For instance, if we speak, we use our ego, and without ego, we can't talk. If we walk, we walk in a specific, personal way, and again our Ego is involved.

After a heart transplant, the murderer of the heart donor could be identified because the girl who received the heart had a vision of the murder. Our organs store the memories, and the memories are part of our ego.

## We cannot guarantee survival without Ego.

We can free ourselves from our egos and connect with the divine for a particular time, yes. With meditation, dancing, music, chanting, and through other techniques this is possible.

If we observe our ego, we can lose our attachments.

## We can't get rid of all our attachments!

We should watch and improve our ego throughout our whole life. And we should forget these so-called enlightenment Masters, Avatars, Divine Incarnations, or Rinpoches. They become arrogant and ignorant of the true purpose of their ego, become greedy, and fall from their spirituality.

The spiritual enlightenment was a great marketing idea to exploit and cheat the people.

The Zen masters even sold enlightenment certificates!

Still, the Enlightenment trip was necessary to motivate, to meditate, and to go farther.

We have heard so many stories from yogis, religious people, monks, and saints, all of whom were secretly having sex when this was explicitly forbidden by their creeds. We wonder why they could not maintain their celibacy and we doubt that they had been divine, holy…

# Is the transformation of our sexuality possible?

Our brain is focused on procreation because nature needs children. What are we if we live in celibacy? We suppress our sex drive with our mind. What we suppress will grow. After some time, our suppressed sexual desire can cause diseases, can become perverted, or it can explode with unstoppable urges for sex. Monks and Nuns suffer double the occurrences of prostate and breast cancer relative to worldly people.

For a healthy life, we need a healthy sex life.

I lived in celibacy for 10 years, and I was in bliss. This was because I had raised my energy from my sex center to my heart or crone chakra and that causes the bliss! Then I had an accident, my back could not heal, and this was because I had suppressed sex. I was able to heal my back with my sex energy (Chi Gong, Mantak Chia).

Do the real Gurus, Masters, Saints, and Rinpoches follow the Divine or their spiritual selves to serve humanity?

# What is the spiritual self, or the divine inner master?

The gurus and serious devotees all have a divine inner master. From this inner master, they receive all the information that is necessary for their own particular spiritual paths. They must obey their spiritual selves 100%. If they follow this rule, they will grow greatly along the spiritual path. If not, they will become evil people and will exploit others - something we see today!

I was fortunate enough to have received Kundalini/spiritual awakening for 29 years. Since then, I have lost my body identification (still, I keep my body healthy), found my divine inner master, and experienced many other spiritual goodies. I have obeyed my true self completely. Sometimes it was/is difficult to follow my spiritual self because I have to do things that are contradictory to my thinking/faith system. Nevertheless, my life got better and better.

Nearly all famous Gurus have exploited and cheated the masses. It is rather the unknown Gurus, like Ramakrishna and Nusrat Fateh Ali Khan, who have been honest and humble.
The great Gurus and Saints put together a beautiful holy show, but those on the inside will tell you how unholy and selfish they are! (See the books referenced about the famous Gurus, written by their dearest devotees, at the end).

I saw Nusrat Fateh Ali Khan only one time, and he gave me a Satory during his concert and changed my life…

Here is the insider information about Osho, for free, packed with all the necessary details: http://meditation-

handbook.50webs.com/osho2.html
Books about Osho: Bhagwan: The God That Failed, by Hugh Milne,
Promise of Paradise: … by Satya Bharti Franklin,
Don't kill him, by Ma Anand Sheela.

About Mata Amritananda Mai Devi: "Holy Hell: A Memoir of Faith,
Devotion, and Pure Madness" by Gail Tredwell

About Sri Chinmoy: "Cartwheel in a Sari" by Jayanti Tamm
and google his sexual abuse…

A book about Maharaji Guru: Without the Guru: How I took my life
back after thirty years, by Dr. Michael Robert Finch (Chauffeur from
Maharaji)

About Sai Baba and his fake materialization and sexual abuse, read:
The Shadow of a God-Man by David Christopher Lane, Ph.D.
Professor of Philosophy, http://www.integralworld.net/lane62.html
About Sai Baba's homosexual abuse of kids and all of his fakery, read:
Hindustan Times: Truth about Satya Sai Baba
http://www.hindustantimes.com/india/truth-about-sathya-sai-
baba/story-BMLoZfl3sJtvW5gr2TeNWO.html
His fake materialization is explained at
https://www.youtube.com/watch?v=VNMxQtwkIuk

Here is the information about the most famous Rinpoches:

A book about Sogyal Rinpoche and his sexual abuse: Lock the door
https://buddhism-controversy-blog.com/2016/12/01/lock-the-door-i-
was-devoted-to-a-great-buddhist-master-and-then-i-quit-by-mimi-
former-dakini/
https://www.theguardian.com/commentisfree/belief/2011/jul/01/lama-
sex-abuse-sogyal-rinpoche-buddhist

Chögyam Trungpa, death by liver cirrhosis through too much alcohol
consumption, Read: https://en.wikipedia.org/wiki/Chögyam_Trungpas

# There exist no Nirvana or Moksha or Mukti

Nirvana or Moksha (Mukti) are terms from Buddhist, Hindu and Jaina Religions. Their definitions are similar.

The idea is that life is sorrow. We get reborn again and again and have to undergo the sorrow until we never get born again. And that is the goal of these 3 Religions.

Everything is Destiny or Karma. We can't change our life… We should stay in our Cast. Everything is predetermined. Be it that we are poor and unsuccessful, and we can't change that. And this awful Idea of fate had made India, Nepal, and Tibet to the poorest Countries in the world. When the Indians skipped this Idea of predestination they became the most successful people in the world. Maybe this is also Destiny. I will prove later that there is also no Karma!

Alone to discontinue to get reborn shows the negative attitude of these Religions!

## Life is sorrow.

## Why is this nonsense?

1. Can you remember your past lives?
2. Even you can remember past lives what has this to do to enjoy your life right now?
3. Without sorrow, we would live in the Stone-Age! Every invention was created to improve our life. At first, the people suffered for something and afterward were created the improvement.
4. First, we suffer and only then we can improve our lives.

76

5. The best times are the worst times. In the worst times, we learn the best things to improve our lives.
6. Remember all of your worst times in your life and find the good things in these worst times. I bet you will find them.
7. Suffering is necessary for a fulfilling life.
8. Have you tried to write on a blackboard with a black pencil? Everything has two pols. We can't enjoy our life if we don't experience sadness, depression. These 3 Religions never could understand the Law of Polarity. The Tao Religion defines the law of polarity.
9. If we don't risk something, we can't change something or make it better. These 3 Religions are afraid to risk something or to go through the polarities.
10. The goal of these Religions is to become a robot without any feelings and thoughts or to be a living corpse. I have seen many Buddhists and Jnani Yogis who were suppressing their emotions, sex, and thoughts. And that should be spiritual growing?
11. The Jaines even fast until they die. That is perverse!
12. Many Yogis even taking drugs,- that should be spiritual growing?
13. In the Buddhist Religion exist two paths the small and the big vehicle. In the small vehicle, only the Monks and Nuns can get Nirvana. In the big vehicle, everybody can reach Nirvana For different Buddhist countries are true the small or big vehicle. It depends on the country where you had been born to get your Nirvana! That makes no sense!

# In the previous chapter, I have proved that our Ego can't be destroyed and so the Nirvana, Moksha or Mukti never had existed.

# There doesn't exist Karma or Justice

Never think over Karma. Because it is indescribable and lead to madness if you over-think it (Buddha). For what we need then a Karma law if it is beyond of our thinking? Religions use the Karma or better our bad Karma to squeeze out the people with their bad consciousness.

The common idea is, you do something good and good is coming back. Can be.

If you are a guy like me, who had a childhood like a hell, you will attract, again and again, the dramas of your childhood. Because we repeat our traumas until we go with full conscious through our traumas.

What has this to do with Karma or Justice?

# It has to do with the Law of Attraction.

The Law of Attraction is working for everybody. We attract what is inside of us, regardless of whether we are aware of it or not.
The law of attraction also involves the law of Karma.
The stronger our feelings are for something that we want, or do not want – the bigger is the attraction.
Our negative emotions are much stronger than our positive ones, so we attract what we:

1. Are afraid of

2. Hate

3. Are angry about

4. Love

5. Want

6. Don't want...

7. Have a Bad conscious of

It makes much more sense for us to focus on the things we do want!

The psychology has proved that we continuously repeat situations/dramas/traumas from our childhood until we have full awareness of it. So the harder our childhood was, the more difficult our lives will be. Even scientists have proved that we manipulate our environment including the people to get the same results that we got in certain situations of our childhood.

If we had significant problems with our mother about our tidiness/or getting angry in a given situation, we are likely to have the same type of challenges as our spouse.

If a woman got raped, the likelihood that she gets raped again is up to 80% after research in London. What has this to do with Karma?

If we steal something and have an evil consciousness about this deed, we attract the police through our fear.

The Vedanta gives us more clues that most people do not understand. If a person steals something and is identified with this deed, then he is the thief. If the individual is not identified, then he is not the doer. -If he is not the doer, then he doesn't attract the punishment.

We can now understand why many wicked people don't attract the struggles that they deserve. Because they are not so identified with their deeds. Like the slaughters and Killers when they kill.

When the dictator Hitler left the scene of the WWII, he married his
girlfriend Eva Braun and moved to Argentina. He never got caught,
the same is true for the past presidents of Thailand, Bin Laden, Assad
(another guy got hanged).  They are too big to punish, like the banks
too big to fail.

# Is there Justice?

I struggled quite a lot when I heard that the best alternative Doctor who was also spiritual from my hometown died in the Tsunami. How can that be, it doesn't make sense! She helped so many sick people, why she had to die and not me in the Tsunami?
I faced also the Tsunami and could prevent to get hurt by the Tsunami.

Imagine you are living in Pakistan on the border with Afghanistan. Every night flyes a Drone over you. On Thursday, the President of the USA gives the commando to kill.
Will you be killed
or is this Karma
or do you think that the people who got killed are worse than us?

When seeing a good dad dying too early, we think he doesn't have deserved that? His family is helpless without him, and maybe we blemish God that God didn't have prevented his death.

Everybody has to care for his own body and should live a healthy lifestyle. There is enough information out, to prevent severe diseases. And this is also true for every good guy!!!!

## God gives us to the right time from inside tips to prevent catastrophes, death, struggles or diseases.

When we are ignorant and don't want to hear that tips coming from inside, or our gut-feelings, then we have deserved the punishment!!!

God is here and only God can protect you if you surrender your life to

God. And with this in mind, who cares for justice, if we know that we are always in Gods hand.

That is good so! That all the other ideas from Karma, security, protection are not working. I have faced in the last 14 years 4 times the death, was 1 time clinical dead (all together I was 3 times clinical dead) and my body was total paralyzed. We don't need a Karma or this blind belief in justice. We need God…

# What is bad about Sex?

1. Judging,- Everything is just so, nor good or bad. We make it bad or good; still, it remains as it is,- neutral.

1. Abusing sex. Every abuse shows our weak side; it shows how much we need sex and doesn't get it, that we are jealous, that we are dishonest.

2. Too much or too less sex harms our body. Monks, nuns have double so often prostate cancer, breast cancer. And too much sex weakens the immune system. What is too much sex? - If we are too drained out through sex.

3. Nearly all women diseases are caused by suppressing and refusing of sex. I went through 136 women diseases for my book (Heal yourself and stay healthy). If the women would enjoy their sex and to be a female; then there would be no reason for females diseases. Why are women getting so punished from nature? Because nature needs children. Essential women are the most remarkable creatures because only they can get children.

4. A shame of sex. Nearly every mutual person has and needs sex; has a sexual drive. So what is special about sex? Why we can't speak over it normal? We just put a stick in a whole, and our phantasm is getting crazy. Why we want to hide it. The Quran says shame is a sign of dishonesty. For instance, in Singapore, a guy posted a picture and a report in the news about their family tradition. The family assisted the son during his first-time intercourse. The readers of this report abused that. I would be happy if the family assisted me when I had my first-time sex. Because I failed and it was so painful to fail in the bed.

5. The guilt of sex. For what is that good? Get rid of it. We are all a product of sex.

6. Not to enjoy sex. Why not enjoy it; sex should be a regular part of our life. Many people are getting fat because they don't live their sex enough. So more corpulent the female body so fewer feelings are in the vagina - science proofed.

7. Frigid,-is psychological (see Impotent) or caused by a dry vagina (oil helps).

8. Impotence,- is caused by the guilt of sex, bad consciousness, and a weak blood circulation. Just, fast for at least one week, or do colon cleaning from the Internet shop Blessed Herbs or sexual organ massage from Mantak Chia. For the psychological reasons make Therapy, Tantra or Tao-love groups.

The Chinese define sex as healthy, and if sex is lost, the immune system is weak. The goal is to have sex until they die. Even with sex, we can cure our diseases if we apply the Techniques of Tao-love (Tao Master Mantak Chia). Actually, I have cured my Spine (broken disk) with it.
I had started very late with intercourse (25 years). After many fail and try in sex, I made Tantra I and Tantra II and I became an expert. I also practice Tao- Love from Mantak Chia.

# Religion and God

# For what we need Religion?

We need Religion:

1. to find inner peace,

2. happiness, love,

3. wisdom,

4. confidence,

5. and to gain faith in ourselves, in the world and in God!

We can't find inner peace when we run behind worldly things.

Is it enough if we meditate and learn to relax even in the difficult times?

If we learn to relax in difficult times with meditation then this is much more than most of all religious people gain in their life!

If we learn religious teaching and spiritual techniques, it is much easier to meditate. We will gain bliss, inner love, inner happiness and to connect with God. Without Religion, we can't understand our life, our world, and we can't connect to the Divine/God.
So that it is priceless to gain meditation with Religion.

Still, we need to understand:

1. ourselves,

2. our psychology,

3. how we act,

4. why we act,

5. how we can change our belief system and subconscious.


I think that psychology is very important to gain what we want.
Without understanding ourselves, every step in a new direction of our
life is much more difficult. This means we need Meditation, Religion,
and Psychology to live a happy life.

# Whatever Religion disapproves is wrong...

Religion is man-made, and God is divine, beyond of our understanding. (Gandhi)

God has no religion. (Gandhi)

Everything has its place (I-Ging, Srimad Bhagavatam, or Esoteric)

And God saw the world and said everything is good.
Or don't fight against the wicked. (Bible)

The Christian, Hindu, Buddhist religion are fighting against the pleasure of sex and the Sufis (Islam Mystic), and Taoist see the sex as divine.

For the Quran is a monastic path of religion wrong and even forbidden. The Quran said the human being is weak, so they should take a spouse.

The Monks and Nuns see an own family as an obstacle to their religious life. Because the religious person can't focus his full attention on God and is even forced to cheat and lie in a sexual relationship.

The Srimad Bhagavatam sees sex in a marriage equal to renounce sex as a yogi. The yogi renounces the world, and the fruits of his doing. The householder renounces inside of himself, the fruits of his doing. Both are the same. The householders should serve their families selflessly, and with that they serve God. The service of the householders to humanity is a great service to God. Without the service of the householders, the Yogis can't live.

# Everything has its place (I-Ging, Srimad Bhagavatam, or Esoteric)

The Srimad Bhagavatam tells us: if one body likes to kill, he should be a soldier. If women love to prostitute they should do so because it serves the needs of men. What is with cheating? They should become businessmen because business is related to cheating (even 5000 years ago). What is with thieving? They should thieve the honey of the bees and sell the honey.

# Nothing is wrong only misplaced!

# For what is the Spiritual Path?

The spiritual path connects us with:

1. God,

2. the Divine,

3. divine happiness,

4. true love,

5. peace in mind,

6. and serenity.

This is only possible if we get disconnected with our ego or mind.

# How can we find this real love, serenity, peace of mind?

The standard methods of the religions are a good starting point. Nevertheless, these methods are not effective enough to get our spiritual outcome. The Religions and the common religious methods should be our foundation to go further. On the other hand, Religion is not necessary to get our spiritual outcome, like peace in mind, real love, serenity or bliss. Still, the combination of Religion, psychology, and spirituality is the best way to get our spirituality.

Spiritual Masters and Mystics designed great techniques, like meditation, Chi-Gong, many different Yoga systems (Kundalini, Bhakti, …), Tantra, Tibetan techniques.

The religious leaders have been against spiritual techniques. Because the individuals became independence happy and fulfilled without the need of the exploiting Religions!

If we read books from Castaneda about the teaching from his master Don Juan, we discover that there is nothing about Religion. Don Juan liked to transform the egos from his disciples and to manipulate their consciousness to a higher plan.

Our ego is in the way to reach a higher plan. We have to work on our ego so that our ego will not block us to go to a higher state. And that is spirituality.

If we go out of our ego or mind, what happens then? Remember an old radio,… if we want to change a channel, we just turn one button in one direction and looking for a new sound signal. We hear first some noise. Still, we turn more and more the button until we have a good signal. The same goes for changing our consciousness state. Psychologist already has discovered 4 different states of the mind Beta, Alpha, Theta, and Delta. There exist many more states of the mind. For instance, the Yogis define the Nivikalpa Samadhi as the highest state of our consciousness.

Fewer gurus can go in Samadhi or can easily leave their egos. Still, they have a normal ego. And they can't get rid of their ego, they can only improve their egos! We need our ego for instance if we like to speak, to eat, to think…

Nevertheless, it is awesome if we could go in Samadhi or if we could choose our consciousness state.

For instance: I can go in bliss, and watch my thoughts or enjoy my bliss and have very fewer thoughts. This I can do everywhere. How I make it? I need only to repeat a name of God and then bliss. Or I pull up my energy from my belly to my heart or I position one hand over my belly and the other hand over my heart, or with the sound of the Chinese numbers loud or remote.

If I focus my energy on my Third Eye, I am very straight and have tremendous power to do what I like. You can learn that too!

Maybe you realize why it is so powerful to learn at least Chi Gong and to get the Kundalini!!!

Still, I have the same problems in life than you!

# What is true Spirituality?

The Religions have owned the spirituality and all other
spirituality are against them! The Religions discriminate spiritual
people who are not in their Religion.

Everybody can gain high spirituality with all kinds of magic without
participating in any Religion. For instance:

1. to levitate,

2. to materialize,

3. to channel information from other souls or from the cosmos,

4. or to be it in Samadhi.

These Spiritual Powers can become great obstacles on the spiritual
path of humility and love.
After some time, the Spiritual Power trips will lead to a devastating
life.
Great was their rise and also great was their fall.

I think we should open our heart to the divine or God and do what
God demands from us. Otherwise, we follow our Ego, regardless how
much spirituality we gain.

Even more, we should develop love to God.

The Buddhist and Jnani Yoga don't have a personal God relationship.
Their Goal is not to feel or think any more. Because they want to
reach Nirvana or Moksha. Even a loving relationship with total
surrender to God is nonsense for them.

After many years the Buddhists Monks and Jnani Yogi have killed their own feelings and passions. What I see is that they have closed their heart and are not open for love and compassion anymore. Most of all Jnani Yogis are over-intellectual and that is a big obstacle on the spiritual path.

What has this to do with true spirituality, to serve and love God selflessly?

Gita Chapter 9:25 Those who worship the demigods will take birth among the demigods; those who worship ghosts and spirits will take birth among such beings; those who worship ancestors go to the ancestors; and those who worship Me will live with Me.

The same is true for the Sufis, who only accept to surrender to God and not to any other spirit.

Moksa and Nirvana are the God of the Buddhists Monk and Jnani Yogi. Because they are focused on them instead to be focused on God!

The Gita says that we should surrender to God otherwise we never get our full potential.

Why should we surrender our life to our EGO Trips when we can choose God?

Think this over,- all the other Goals in our life are obstacles to focus on God. Never the less we have worldly desires and we should live the important Goals. And then we focus on God again without demanding Moksha, Enlightenment, Nirvana, Paradise or anything else!

If I love you and demand something back from you then this is not love! For instance, a woman says she loves you and she wants money for sex,- is this Love?

If we love God, we don't want something back! Rather more we are thankful for what we have.

# What is God?

I saw a video from a very talented Kid who was describing God.
He could not understand that you never can discover God with your
rational mind. Because God is beyond of it.

God is beyond of our thinking and is present in total love. Because
God is Love and Love is God. Who can describe Love? If we feel
love, we feel only our resistance to love. We are in a space of Love
when: everything is so beautiful that we can't describe it and
When we can embrace everything.

People who had been in the war saw the light or better divine light on
the battlefield in the most dangerous situation of their life. The same
came true for the Sister and Brother Scholl when they were waiting
for their execution for the attempt to kill Adolf Hitler. In their last 10
days, many people had witnessed that the Scholls had been radiating
so much love and light. And nobody could provoke them.

Or if we go to an African Church when a healer is conducting a
worship for Jesus. The Africans sing with so much surrender and
beautiful voices to Jesus, they dance like crazy for Jesus; that Jesus
can't resist and is coming as a spirit. I could witness that. Even as a
Non-Christ, Jesus was also coming to me. The Formula is the total
surrender to God with Love. Tip: You find African Churches
everywhere in the world.

We can't experience God, without spiritual practice/ or complete faith.
God is not for Free!  Then to speculate with the mind, God doesn't
exist, because I can't see him is nonsense. We need total surrender to
see the divine light or God.
Read later: Why I believe in God.

# Why is it so important to have a God relationship for our life/love/happiness?

If we build up a personal God relationship, then God will help us for our meditation, spirituality and whole life. God will give us at the right time through our intuition the information to prevent disasters, accidents, diseases, and the death. – That is priceless.

If we don't build up a personal God relationship, how can God help us? If we love God then God will help us. But if we ignore God then he can't help us, because we are not open to God.

God loves to help us. If we address God as an impersonal being by using words such as the divine, existence, or universe he will ignore us. By addressing Him with these words, we push God away from us. Firstly, it is very unfriendly and impolite and secondly how can we expect that God will help us.

Imagine,

A. I address you nice and friendly with your name and ask for your help.

B. Or I ask you without mention your name using even can he/she help me.

What will work better A or B?

The next reason is that God is also Satchitananda, which means Absolute Consciousness Bliss or Love. If we concentrate on something then eventually we can become it. If we love somebody we always think about them. If we always think about God we develop love to God. What you love, you become eventually.

This is the reason that my focus point is God in my meditation.

The journey begins when we start a personal relationship with God. So that we feel that there is somebody we can relate to.

A normal prayer that we repeat again and again will never help us much. Actually, I never have done it, I don't pray, because of Osho, my first Guru, was totally against it.

We communicate with God like we communicate with a spouse/friend or with our parents. That is what I do! Where there is love, there is God, or love is God. (Bible).

If we sing with great devotion songs for God, then miracles can happen.

# What have the Disasters to do with God?

We cannot blame God/Allah for any disaster or bad luck. Because we are responsible for our life.

A Guru taught faith. His disciples went into the jungle to collect wood. A wild elephant troop encountered them. One disciple didn't run away, instead were facing the wild elephants. The other disciples were calling him: Go! But he didn't move. The elephants run over him. After he recovered, the Guru asked him: "Why didn't you run away?"

The disciple said: "I have Faith in God"

The Master asked: "Could you do not hear God shouting: Go, through the mouths of ours?"

If we are open, we see, hear and recognize the warning for a disaster quite before it happened.

The world has his cycles/mechanics, and they run without that God interferes.

If we are open to our intuition, we get the warnings. For the religious people like Bob Proctor, is the intuition the answer of God.

# For what we need God?

People who were challenging big catastrophes with all the
nightmares/traumas could recover much faster if they had a positive
belief.

(After a research from Hurricane Katharina)

A positive belief is, that you give "thank you" to God that you have
survived, still alive, enough to eat.

A negative belief is, that you think, God wants to punish you or the
people for their sins. Or the devil had done it.

With a positive belief, we go much easier through our life. We know
that we don't have anything under our control and trust God. That
God knows it much better than us what is the best for us and that "his
will" will happen. He will give us at the right moment what we need
and not necessarily what we want. We find inside of us peace just
through our belief in God.

God is love, and if we surrender to God, we become what we
surrender to.

If we want to gain something, we have to do also the work. If we want
to win the Highest/ Best, we have to do a lot more. And this comes
true for the inner path, belief, and trust in God. In the worst time of
our life, we develop love and faith in God/Allah.

# Why I believe in God?

Let me tell something from me: I was growing up as an atheist and my family was not baptized for centuries. My father' s family was free mansion for 300 years. God was for me taboo; it was not allowed to go to the church or to worship God.

After my 2nd near death experience with 21years, I experienced that there is no death. I questioned my life and found a new Goal in my life. My life should be the sum of my happiness. I started with inquiring myself, yoga, qigong, and meditation.

I became a disciple of Bhagwan/Osho and got the name: Ghanshyam, a name for God, or to be an answer for God. I was complaining about this name because I was an atheist.

I attended many self-experience groups, like Primal, Encounter, Bioenergetic, Meditation, and Tantra workshops. Soon, I became fast spiritual when I learned and practice the sexual Tantra, and got in love with my soul mate. During our 10 weeks together, we had such high spiritual experience that I experience a part of God. And my spirituality went through the roof.

I became thirsty for God and started with Kundalini exercises together with my friend. Both of us got the Kundalini.

Afterward, I started with long meditation retreats of 9 months. After my second retreat, I visited a concert with the Sufi Nusrat Fateh Ali Khan, and he connected me more to God. I got a Satori from him.

I renounce my worldly life, moved to India and meditated in the presence of Mata Amritanada Mai. I was over 12 years in Meditation retreats and over 10 years in celibacy.

After an accident, I could not meditate anymore and moved to

Thailand. Cured my back with Qigong, Acupuncture, and massage. In the meantime, many miracles happened to me. And through the grace of God, I am still alive and healthy.

For instance, I was attacked by 5 young Guys with a pistole in Brasilia and within 2 minutes they were escaping because Mother Kali helped me.

Then, 3 years ago my whole body was paralyzed that was even worse than to be clinical dead. My brain had too less oxygen through a heart rhythmic attack. No chance anymore. During the whole time, I was repeating the name of the Lord and gave thank you to God, that I am still alive and for my awesome life. I remembered the movie "The Secret" and visualized to go by myself out of the hospital. After 7 hours, I did so.

# True Religion

The basis of a true Religion are:

**1. Honesty:**

Honesty, regardless what matter it is. The Great Saint Ramakrishna said: he never can sacrifice his honesty, regardless what. Or Ramakrishna said: when he sees a totally honest person he knows that this is his last life.

Gandhi said: You can not hurt me without that I have given you the permission.

The Hindu and Buddhist Religion are wrong because we should not hurt people with the truth or tell the trues about the fake Gurus!

We are blind to our own errors and shortcomings. Only, when somebody is pointing out that we are wrong we can comprehend. Or remember the story of the King without cloth, when a child said the king has no clothing on, the king realized that he was naked.

Quotes: One honest word is more than 1000 flatter words. Honesty hurts (it should be).

**2. Health:**

In a healthy body is also a healthy soul!

For the Sufis is the body the temple of God. For the Taoist are health and longevity a must!

If we get ill then there is a reason for that. It might be an unhealthy lifestyle or suppressed negative feelings. In any case, we should know:

1. why we live an unhealthy lifestyle,

2. or why we suppress our negative feelings, and

3. which feelings we have suppressed in which situation?

Read my book: "Heal yourself and stay healthy!"

## 3. Live your sex:

The Sufis are saying that sex is divine and similar is it to the Taoists. We should live our sex otherwise suppressed sex leads to diseases or perversions. Monks and nuns have double so much prostate cancer and breast cancer than worldly people. If our sex life is too exhausting, we should reduce our sex. Because too much and too less sex harms our body.

## 4. Personal God relationship:

We should develop a personal God relationship and have faith in God. If we do so our life will be much easier and we can develop our spirituality much faster.

## 5. Awareness:

Awareness of our feelings, thoughts and of the changes in the world is necessary to live a religious life. Aristotle: (Ignorantia Juris nonexcusat) Ignorance does not protect one from punishment.

## 4. Love and compassion:

Love and compassion are the highest goods in the world. Love is the sum of our good habits (Tao) and should be based on honesty and health!

## 5. Never give blind faith to anybody.

No religious or worldly leader should be idealized, rather more checked again and again, for his honesty. Ramakrishna said: Please check me like counterfeit money.
Osho said: You are responsible for your life and for your decisions. Blind faith will never help you! You should be the driver of your life and be aware what you are doing. Don't give blind faith to me or anybody else!

## 6. No corruption...

Every income and every spending should be taxed.

The government should:

- check the tax,

- regulate every temple, monastery, church, and mosque, to make sure that never corruption will happen again.

Every misuse or corruption should be punished with the highest penalty. Because people have donated selflessly their hard-earned money to the religious organizations. Their donations were to help the poor and needy people, money for catastrophes.... The Religions have misused their money.

For instance, the Thai Military government checks for corruption every temple. And every temple has to pay tax on their income. The government checks the income of the temples. Every Religion should do so.

## 7. No Politics of Religion.

The Religions should only teach religion, help the poor and needy people and don't make politics!

# How to develop a Love Relationship with God?

What makes a great intimate relationship?

1. We can share all of our feelings and thoughts with our partner, regardless of what feelings and thoughts we have.

2. If we want to truly connect with somebody, we connect with our feelings.

3. Feelings are what really matter in an intimate relationship.

## Uncultivated people beat and abuse their Gods. Cultivated people are adoring God and making wars! (Sri Aurobindo (in his aphorism))

When Kamsa got killed by Krishna, his soul went to heaven.

The people asked Krishna: "Why did this have to happen? Kamsa was such a wicked guy and had tried again and again to kill you!"

Krishna said, "Kamsa was one of my best devotees. He was hating me so much so that he was thinking about me 24 hours a day nonstop. And Kamsa thought with such great focus on me."

Please understand that human beings can hate up to 5 to 10 times more than they can love.

The focus of your sentiments is what matters if you worship me! (Srimad Bhagavatam).

# If you honor God or if you are afraid of God how can you love God?

(By Attar, one of the greatest Sufi wrote this in his famous book: "Conference of the birds".)

## How we develop love to God?

1.      The journey begins when we start a personal relationship with God. We feel that there is somebody we can relate to. A normal prayer that we repeat again and again will never help us much. Actually, I never have prayed. I don't pray, because of Osho, my first Guru, was totally against it. We communicate with God like we communicate with a spouse/friend or with our parents. That is what I do!

2.      We build up an intimate relationship with God if we see God as the one who is doing everything. The Hindu scripture says everything that is created, or moves, is the action of God, and without God, nothing can happen. We give God the responsibility for everything, good or bad. Here comes the trick! We also have the right to beat up and to abuse God for the bad things that have happened or are happening to us. I know what you are thinking, in the end, everything happens for a reason, and we should be fully responsible for our life. But in this case, it is not helping us. If we release our negative

sentiments, the positive feelings will come. That is proved
through the encounter groups or the law of polarity.

3.        In the end, you will love God. You will understand that
everything was for the best. This time you really feel it! We
chant a name (your pet name for God) of God and repeat the
name during the day as often as possible. In the meditation, we
repeat a name of God.

Attar described, again and again, the example of great human love and
didn't discriminate so much between a great human love and love with
God. Attar saw that an outstanding human love was a must to develop
a love with God.

# At first, build the relationship with God and then start with Japa (repetition of the name of God) otherwise Japa will not work!

## Singing devotional Songs for God as a meditation

When I was in India I recognized that singing for God is at least equal
to meditation. Even Osho said that if there could be only one choice
between music or meditation, he would choose music. With music, we
can directly change our mood and the mood of our friends.

Though, not all music is good. If we hear music with bad lyrics this
will definitely negatively influence our subconscious, as well as our

conscious mind and body. The idea of singing devotional songs for God is that we express our feelings for God and then miracles really can happen!

When I was attending Christian worships at an African Church in Germany, real miracles like spontaneous healing or great spiritual experiences during singing was quite common. I can never sing as beautiful as the Africans in that church, but it doesn't matter. The important thing was that I surrendered totally to sing for Jesus so that Jesus was coming to me, even though I was never in this life a Christian.

This is the point - don't be shy about singing for God. Singing devotional songs isn't for enhancing the EGO!

# More from the Author

I really hope that I could help you to find inner peace, to enjoy more of your life… Thank you for the reading of my book. I have written four more books in English, Enjoy your life now! http://www.amzn.com/B012DFPHJ8 , Learn to Relax with Meditation. https://www.amazon.com/dp/B01561ZWBO ), Heal yourself and stay healthy!   http://www.amzn.com/B016BJPXXC  The Essence to Become Happy, Healthy and Successful! http://www.amzn.com/B06XWYL6WF . The Magic or Qigong. http://amzn.com/B0759PJVF8
 When you click on them, you can see and buy them on Amazon. In the back of this book, you find the description.

I have also created an online Meditation course on YouTube…. For free.

Go to my channel, here you find the Meditation course.

 https://www.youtube.com/c/RudiZimmerer

As a self-publishing author, most of my reviews come directly from readers. It would mean a lot to me if you left a review for this book. Thank you very much for reading my work!

Subscribe to my Newsletter: Relax with Meditation. This is a Newsletter about Spirituality, Psychology, Religion, Health… Here you get two times a week good insights, and you can connect with me and ask a question.

 https://ask-rudy.com/newsletter/

Have an awesome day

Rudi

PS: If you like to be in my Facebook Group: Relax With Meditation then click here.

( https://www.facebook.com/groups/RelaxWithMeditation/ )

If you have an Ipod, connect with my Channel: Relax with Meditation
https://itunes.apple.com/us/podcast/relax-with-meditation/id1245179712?mt=2

# My other Books:

# Enjoy Your Life Now!

### How to Become Happy and Successful with powerful techniques from East and West.

1. I have compiled in over 30 years the most efficient techniques to find true happiness and true love.
2. How to change your life in every aspect with feelings and body-orientated therapy combined with meditation.

1. **How to get back the love** or connection you may not have received as a child.
2. **How to feel true love** in all your relationships.
3. How to have more fulfilling relationships.

4. How to deal with problems when you are working.
5. **How to live a fulfilled life** even when many things are running against you.
6. Learn that we manifest in our lives what is inside of us regardless if we are aware of it or not.
7. What is true happiness, true love, and true meditation?
8. You will learn the most effective EFT.
9. You will learn why meditation and body exercise is so necessary for living a fulfilled life.
10. And much more you find in my book: Enjoy your life now.


Buy this book from Amazon.
https://amzn.com/B012DFPHJ8

# Learn to Relax with Meditation
## How to gain Bliss & Inner Peace with the Energy

Most people don't understand that meditation reflects what is inside of us. When we are fighting against our thoughts, sometimes we don't even know that our suppressed feelings have caused the thoughts. This book shows:

1. how to release negative emotions with EFT;
2. how to gain bliss with the energy pump;
3. how to ground negative thoughts so that they disappear;
4. how God can benefit our meditation and life;
5. how we can learn to love God;
6. how we can use Tantra and Tao love to gain great results fast for

our meditation and spirituality and to enjoy our sexuality;
7. how to achieve health through releasing negative suppressed
feelings, the right food, and through the Chi Gong exercises.


**Buy this book from** *Amazon* .  https://www.amzn.com/B01561ZWBO

# Heal Yourself And Stay Healthy!

Learn The Cause Of Diseases And How To Heal Diabetes, Cancer, Heart, Back...

I have written this book, because of so many wrong concepts for healing the body... I want to help you, to get your health back, in easily doable steps and as fast as possible. I want that you enjoy your life because I know how hard it is to suffer from diseases, to lose all of our hopes.

Do you want to heal your heart, cancer, your back, diabetes and 140 other diseases? Then this book is for you. Even more, I describe how to live a healthy life with good food, body exercise, and Chi Gong. I describe the best Chi Gong exercises and give you the best addresses or links for healing that I have found in this book.

**Learn The Cause Of Diseases**
- *psychosomatic or weak immune system-*
**And How To Heal Diabetes,**

**Cancer, Heart, Back...**

Health and Fitness Expert
Rudi Zimmerer

In my book I describe:

Before you heal your body heal first your soul.
The cause of diseases are suppressed feelings, stress, unhealthy food,
western medicaments, too less exercise, too less sleep and rest.

1. Why we treat our body so bad with unhealthy food, overeating, not
      enough exercise, too much stress…?
2. Why is faith the most important thing in our healing?
3. Why is fear or no faith in the healing the worst?
4. Why can't Western medicine give us health and weakens our body?
5. Why we need a healthy lifestyle, with healthy food such as fresh
      juices, sprouts, green smoothies and time for rest, relaxation
      and body exercise?

You find the answers in this book.

I had suffered many years from my epilepsy, back and knee problems,
weak immune system, heart problems. I tried out many healing
concepts… Many didn't work… In the last 40 years. I healed myself
and other from severe diseases.

Some reviews:  Great book for a diabetic!
          Get healthy and stay healthy with the book!

Buy this book from Amazon   http://www.amzn.com/B016BJPXXC

# The Essence to Become Happy, Healthy and Successful!

## From my Facebook Group: Relax with Meditation

In this book, I include the best for our happiness, health, success and spirituality in easily consumable portions from my Facebook Group: Relax with Meditation. There are 140 articles quick to read and to understand. Just open the book somewhere, read one article, relax and improve your life. You don't have to read the whole book, just one article at a time ... is enough. I found a great article from the very successful Man Dr. Patrick Liew (Co-Founder Success Resources), "How to re-craft our life?" I asked him, to use this material for my book, and he also wrote the foreword.

**Rudi Zimmerer**
International Meditation Master

The *Essence* to become
Happy, Healthy and Successful!
From my  GR: Relax With Meditation

In my book I describe:

1. Why we don't get what we want?

2. How to Overcome Procrastination?

3. What is an optimal time management?

4. How to get our life back?

5. How to get rid of our Anger?

6. How to become creative?

7. How to improve our relationships?

8. How to become Forever Young?

9. What is the best for our Immune system!

10. What are the causes of all diseases and the cure?

11. How to cure cancer?

12. What is the meaning of our life?

13. Is there more?

14. What is God?

15. Why is it so important to have a God relationship?

16. I can't die, I am Energy... ?

17. Is There A Free Will?

18. Fake Gurus - True Gurus?

**Buy this book from Amazon . http://www.amzn.com/B06XWYL6WF**

# The Magic of Qigong!

## With the Immortal Qigong,
## Fulfilling Bliss and Tao-Love.

Qigong Master Rudi Zimmerer

The Magic of Qigong!
With the Immortal Qigong,
Fulfilling Bliss and Tao-Love.

In this book, you will learn the most efficient Qigong. You will discover all the secrets of Qigong that never had been published in one book before. And you need only one hour per day to become healthy and vigor. With the Immortal Qigong is long levity over 100 years possible.

This book teaches you:

1. Do You want to release fast and efficient your negative emotions? With the Tao 5 Elements and the Healing Sounds, you can do so.

2. Do You want to balance your Energy in your body? With Tao Two

Hand Method and the Healing Sounds, you can do so.

3. Do You want Peace in your mind and experience Bliss? With my moving Qigong, you will gain that and excellent Health.

4. Do You want to Live Long and to be Healthy and Vigor? With the Immortal Qigong from Lu Zijian (Lu Zijian died with 118 and was vigor and healthy until his end), you achieve that, and you will get Bliss and Peace in mind.

5. Do You want to Enjoy Your Sex, to have a longer Climax and even to Heal our body? With the Tao-Love, you do so.

6. Do you have problems to learn new things? You can easily learn my Qigong with my videos. For free, You can download and see my Qigong videos.

Buy this book from Amazon . http://amzn.com/B0759PJVF8

# Give your life a meaning or enjoy…

Consider please:

Nothing has a meaning until we give it a meaning.

If we would enjoy our entire life, we don't need a meaning for our life.

Most people can't enjoy their life even they can't enjoy their working time… I will help you in this book to enjoy your entire life!

Still, we should give our life a meaning that will direct our life. So that we know why we do this and not waste our time for meaningless things…

You find the answers in this book.

1. Why can't we enjoy our life?

2. Why are good relationships more important than wealth and success?

3. Why should we care for our intimacy relationships?

4. Why do we need to enjoy our Job?

5. Why do we need a goal setting?

6. Why can't we rely on our kids as the meaning of life?

7. Why should we fulfill our heart desires?

8. Why is it essential to have a mission?

9. Why should we stop regretting instead to do it?

10.    Why should we learn to go beyond our desires?

11.    Why do we need to be connected with God/divine?

12.    Why can God/Divine give us a meaning of life?


Buy this book from Amazon   https://www.amzn.com/B07NLM3MS9

# Have Faith in the Lord

## This book describes in many stories how you can gain Faith in God.

I have written this book for God, to promote Faith in God.
All stories inside of this book are authentic life stories from myself.
I start with my situation right now, the dramatical healing of terminal colon cancer of my girlfriend through Faith in the Lord!

And then I tell how the Lord saved my life again and again. I explain: How to gain love and faith in God in every religion. As a bonus I give insights: Does exist the: Kundalini; Enlightenment;

life after death; Moksha; Paradise or Hell? In this book are no hidden ads or promotions.
https://ask-rudy.com/faith

**Buy this Book from Amazon**

**https://www.amzn.com/B091CX4GQ9**

# Back cover

This book is written for people who are frustrated from the Organized Religions and the spiritual Masters. People who like to connect with God and don't like to obey stupid rules of the Religions.

**You will learn:**

1. That the organized Religions are just another Spam!
2. Why don't exist Paradise and Hell?
3. Why don't exist Nirvana, Moksha, and Enlightenment?
4. It doesn't exist a final death -science proofed by the Research done on 996 people.
5. The worst and cruelest verses of the Quran and the Bible.
6. The Quran encourages to enslave, kill, rape and torture Nonbelievers of the Islam.
7. What is God?
8. How important is it to have a personal God relationship?
9. How to connect to God?
10.     That sex is good and healthy.